Discover Doncaster!

Second edition - now with added time travel!

www.philshepp.com

Photographs kindly provided by Doncaster Tourism, Doncaster Museum and The History Press (pages 24-25).

This is Jay.
She loves geography.

Here's Harry.
He's into
history.

And this is Donny.
He likes...
well, he just likes eating!

teacher's voice

...and today, your homework will be...

Fingers crossed for history

Geography geography

...the history **and** geography of...

...Doncaster!

Doncaster? Really?

Surely there's nothing interesting about Doncaster!

CARETAKER

Hey kids! I've finally finished fixing that middle toilet! Come and take a look!

Mr Snapper the caretaker

Contents

I've made a few adjustments. It is now...

...a time-travelling toilet! Let's GO-O-O!

And so, Harry, Jay and Donny visited Doncaster's past. Here's what they found out...

Where in the world?

England is part of the United Kingdom, which is found in the **continent** of Europe.

PREHISTORIC DONCASTER

After an Ice Age, the warming of the climate led settlers to the Doncaster area about 10,000 **BC**. Stone age hunter gatherers used local caves for shelter and as bases for hunting. They produced tools, blades and axes from flint, a type of hard stone. A number of these tools have been discovered in the Doncaster area over the years, just like this stone spear head...

CRAZY FACT! Doncaster was seized by the Scots in 1136 – and may nev

Our country is split into various **counties**.
Doncaster is in the county of South Yorkshire...

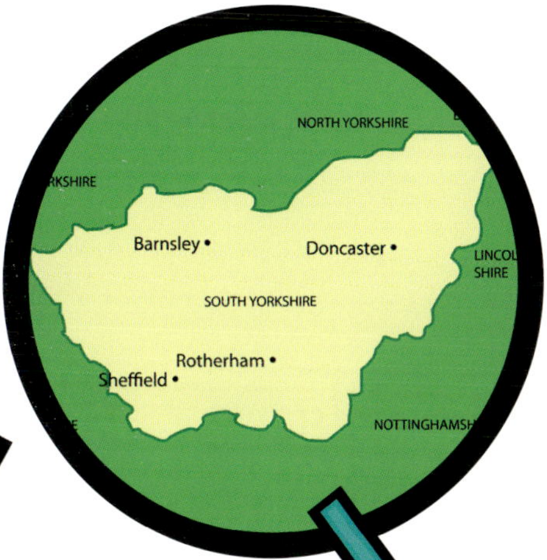

NORTH YORKSHIRE

RKSHIRE

Barnsley •

Doncaster •

LINCOL
SHIRE

SOUTH YORKSHIRE

Rotherham •
Sheffield •

NOTTINGHAMSH

The **borough** of
Doncaster is then
split into smaller
towns, villages
and suburbs
such as Thorne,
Conisbrough,
Finningley and
Mexborough.

MAP

Stainforth and
Moorends

Askern Spa

Adwick

Edenthorpe
Kirk Sandall
& Barnby
Dun

Hatfield

Thorne

Bentley

Sprotbrough

Great
North
Road

Wheatley

Town
Moor

Armthorpe

Central

Finningley

Mexborough

Balby

Conisbrough
& Denaby

Edlington &
Warmsworth

Rossington

Torne Valley

HORRIBLE DONCASTER

Bog bodies in Doncaster!

Parts of Doncaster have a type of
rich soil called **peat**. In 1747, a man
accidentally dug up... a human arm!
It belonged to a body that had been preserved in the peat bog –
just like an Egyptian mummy! It was reported that the skin "was
yellowy brown like leather, the bones were black and the hair firm
on his head". Two more bodies were discovered and dated back to
the 1st Century **AD**... our ancient Doncaster **ancestors**!

ave officially been handed back! So is Doncaster still actually part of SCOTLAND?

Can you spot it?

Next time you are in Doncaster, see if you can spot these famous landmarks...

Clock corner

The Corn Exchange

FACT! The **composer** Sir Edward Elgar conducted the London Symphony Orchestra here in 1909.

The Mansion House

FACT! There are only three mansion houses in the UK!

The Dome

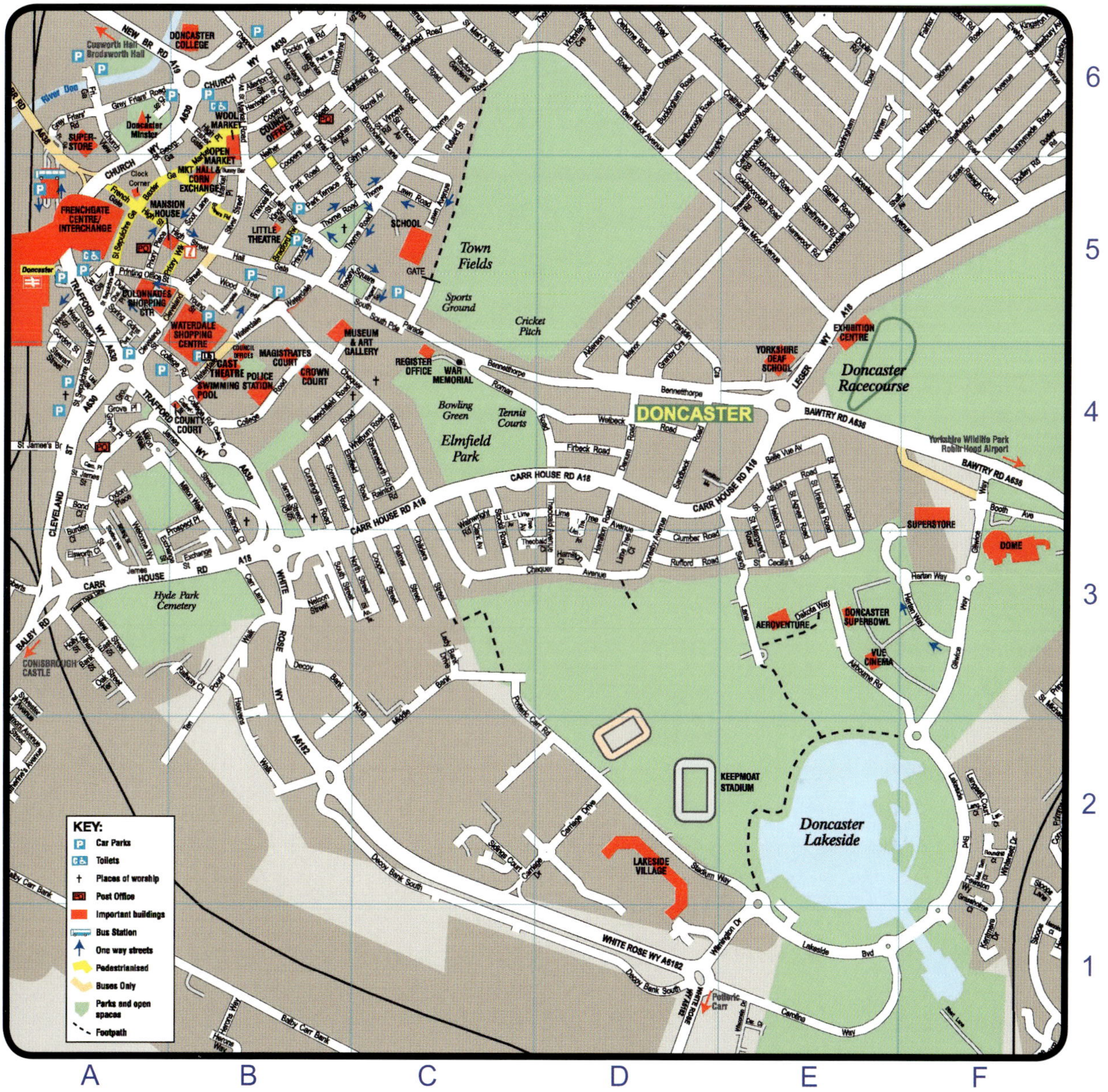

Map of Doncaster

Grid references (top to bottom): 6, 5, 4, 3, 2, 1

Grid references (left to right): A, B, C, D, E, F

KEY:
- **P** Car Parks
- **C&T** Toilets
- **+** Places of worship
- **P.O.** Post Office
- Important buildings
- Bus Station
- **↑** One way streets
- Pedestrianised
- Buses Only
- Parks and open spaces
- - - Footpath

Map labels include:
NEW BR RD, DONCASTER COLLEGE, CHURCH WY, WOOL MARKET, COUNCIL OFFICES, DONCASTER MINSTER, SUPER-F STORE, OPEN MARKET, MKT HALL & CORN EXCHANGE, MANSION HOUSE, Clock Corner, FRENCHGATE CENTRE/INTERCHANGE, Doncaster, COLONNADES SHOPPING CTR, WATERDALE SHOPPING CENTRE, LITTLE THEATRE, SCHOOL, Town Fields, GATE, Sports Ground, Cricket Pitch, MAGISTRATES COURT, CAST THEATRE, CROWN COURT, POLICE STATION, SWIMMING POOL, MUSEUM & ART GALLERY, REGISTER OFFICE, WAR MEMORIAL, Bowling Green, Tennis Courts, Elmfield Park, **DONCASTER**, YORKSHIRE DEAF SCHOOL, EXHIBITION CENTRE, Doncaster Racecourse, BAWTRY RD A638, Yorkshire Wildlife Park, Robin Hood Airport, CARR HOUSE RD A18, SUPERSTORE, DOME, Harlan Way, St James's Br, CLEVELAND ST, Hyde Park Cemetery, AEROVENTURE, DONCASTER SUPERBOWL, VUE CINEMA, CONISBROUGH CASTLE, BALBY RD, CARR, WHITE ROSE WY, KEEPMOAT STADIUM, Doncaster Lakeside, LAKESIDE VILLAGE, WHITE ROSE WY A6182, Decoy Bank South, Potteric Carr

QUIZ! Look at the map above. What are the grid references for places on these pages? Answers on page 8...

Doncaster Racecourse

7

The Romans

Doncaster was very important to the Romans. The town was built on the site of a Roman **fort** in the 1st century AD at a crossing of the River Don.

Constantine the Great, the first Christian Emperor of Rome, sent his son Crispin to live here, and Doncaster became home to the Roman Crispinian **horse garrison**.

Famously, the Romans linked their forts with long, straight roads, many of which we still use today.

What's in a name?

The Romans called their fort "Danum" as it meant 'by the river'. This is where our town gets the "Don-" part of its name. "Caster" is an Old English word, meaning an army camp. *Put them together and what do you get...?*

Dig dig dig!

Nowadays, Doncaster is very interesting to **archaeologists**, with many Roman areas hidden under buildings. St George's Minster is believed to cover the old Roman fort. If you visit the Minster, you can find the remains of a Roman wall yourself! Some people believe that there is a Roman burial ground under the Frenchgate Centre too. Think about that next time you're shopping there!

The Romans built walls up to 2 metres thick!

Danum Shield – the first Roman shield of its type found anywhere and named after Doncaster.

There is lots of Roman stuff at Doncaster Museum... as well as a few old bones. Yummy!

The River Don

The River Don is a very important part of Doncaster. The Romans set up camp next to its banks, meaning the beginning of our town. Since then it has been vital for local **industry**, transporting goods and helping make Doncaster the central hub it is today.

Doncaster's main bridge across the River Don is called St George's Bridge. Not far away is St George's Gate. This is where petty criminals used to be put into the **stocks**. Passers-by were encouraged to throw mud, rotten eggs, mouldy fruit and vegetables, smelly fish and excrement (that's poo - both animal and human!) at those being punished.

When **Henry VIII** broke from the Catholic Church, there was an angry uprising called 'The Pilgrimage of Grace'. Between thirty and forty thousand people headed south through Doncaster to deal with Henry. Luckily for him, on the night of 26 October 1536, the River Don flooded, stopping the forces from crossing at Doncaster. This forced them to negotiate with Henry.

Thanks River Don! Cheers!

The River Don rises in the **Pennines** and flows for 70 miles (110 km) eastwards, through the Don Valley.

It used to suffer pollution problems due to local industry, but efforts to improve the water quality and **habitats** have met with some success, with salmon now spotted near Doncaster!

Conisbrough Castle

Conisbrough Castle still has the finest circular keep tower in the whole of the UK. It was built by the 4th Earl of Surrey (the half-brother of King Henry II) in Norman times.

HORRIBLE DONCASTER

Some believe that Conisbrough Castle has its very own ghost!

A spooky "White Lady" has been seen at the top of the keep, where she is said to have been pushed over the edge to her death. It has been claimed that she is the ghost of Countess de Warrenne, who some say was murdered by her husband in the castle chapel. What do you believe?

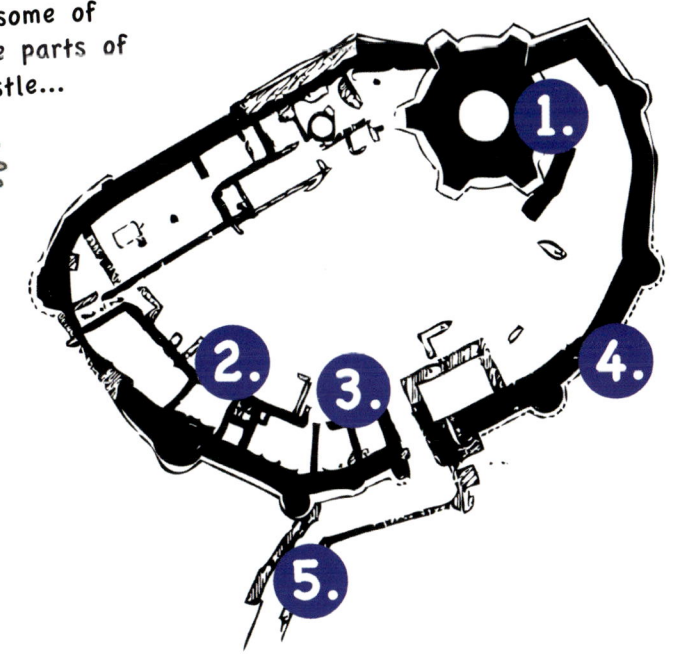

Here are some of my favourite parts of the castle...

1. The Keep

The Keep is the oldest part of the castle, dating back to 1180. It is 27 metres high with walls 4.6 metres thick. If the castle came under attack, the defenders would retreat to the Keep, pull in the wooden bridge and bolt the door, making it almost impossible for the attackers to get in.

2. The Latrine Pit

'Latrine' is another name for a toilet! People did their business down a hole, then it would slide down a chute into this pit, which had to be emptied by hand. Urgh!

3. A prison cell was located through a trapdoor under the guardhouse floor.

4. Fallen South Wall

This wall fell during the reign of Henry VIII, so the castle was 'closed down' and became a ruin. Although this sounds like a terrible thing, it meant that the castle was left alone during the English Civil War of the 1640s, not destroyed like most others. Phew!

5. The Barbican

A trap! The first **portcullis gate** would be opened, letting attackers in easily. But once they were inside, it was dropped shut! A second gate at the top of the passage would have been closed from the start, trapping the attackers inside! Soldiers would then shoot arrows or drop missiles through "Murder Holes" in the Gatehouse above, killing their trapped victims!

13

Doncaster Market

Doncaster Market is one of the oldest and most well-known in the country.

Can you spot it?

A pig on a pole? Where in the market will you see this statue? And which animal is stood on the pole opposite?

There would have almost certainly been a market in Doncaster during Roman times. Then, during Tudor times in 1505, King Henry VII granted Doncaster the right to hold a market every Tuesday and Saturday - and we have been busy selling and buying in the same historic market ever since.

The main building in the market is called the 'Corn Exchange'. It was built in 1873 and rebuilt in 1994 after a major fire.

14

HORRIBLE DONCASTER

The 1600s saw the royalist Cavaliers fight the rebel Roundheads in England's Civil War. When Colonel Rainsborough, a leading Roundhead, stayed at an inn in Doncaster market, Cavaliers secretly entered the town pretending to have a letter for him. A trick! They tried to take him prisoner, but Rainsborough struggled and was run through with a sword... **murdered**!

Fact or Fiction?

It was Richard the Lionheart who granted Doncaster its first market charter. But what of Robin Hood, who is said to have robbed from the rich in the name of King Richard? Research places the outlaw in Barnsdale, near Doncaster - not in Sherwood Forest as famously thought. At least that is what the people at Doncaster's Robin Hood Airport claim! What do you think?

Statue at Robin Hood Airport

Victorian Doncaster

Queen Victoria ruled from 1837 until her death in 1901. During her reign, Britain went through some great changes, and many of Doncaster's buildings were built during this time.

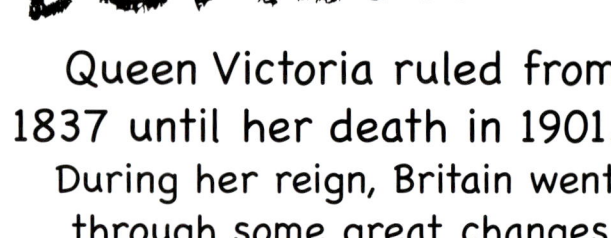

ABOVE: This portrait of Queen Victoria is in the Doncaster Mansion House.

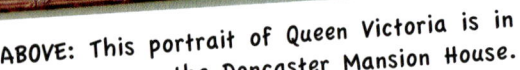

DONCASTER STAR Thomas Crapper

Thomas Crapper was famous for making toile Born in Thorne in 1836, Crapper introduced the 'ball-cock' to make them flush easily. He also invented the bathroom showroom and a spring-action toilet seat they called 'the bottom slapper' (that one didn't catch on).

Can you spot a black silouette of a loo in this Hatfield church window? It's a tribute to Crapper.

Do you like sweets? So did Queen Victoria! Butterscotch was invented by Samuel Parkinson in 1817 in Doncaster. It was presented as a gift to Queen Victoria on her visit to Doncaster in 1855 and she soon requested supplies "by royal appointment".

Can you spot it?

PARKINSONS MAKERS OF DONCASTER BUTTERSCOTCH OCCUPIED THIS SHOP 1817-1960 DONCASTER CIVIC TRUST

Shhh! Here's a little-known part of Doncaster's history...

The Sand House

Victorian businessman Henry Senior was a marvellous man indeed. He carved his own mansion into a solid block of sandstone at his quarry, then dug tunnels nearby. The tunnels were full of weird and wonderful statues, carved into the walls themselves.

Unfortunately, the Sand House is now the location of a block of flats... but some say that parts of the tunnels still exist.

Could you be above them right now?

17

The Minster Church of Saint George

It was medieval times when the first church was built on the site of our minster. By 1430 AD, its tower stood at 141 feet above the surrounding countryside. That is as tall as eight giraffes! It was the pride of the town.

Can you spot it?

ANIMAL SPECIAL!

The Minster is full of hidden animals...

...like this catapillar carved into the stone!

But, on the night of 28th February 1853, disaster struck! A terrible fire destroyed the building. This was seen as a great calamity for the town... but they bounced back, starting work on a new church just one week later!

Even Queen Victoria broke her own rule not to contribute to local charities and gave £100 to the fund.

Victorian stained glass.

18

The clock at Doncaster Minster was designed and made by the same men that made 'Big Ben' in London: Lord Grimthorpe and John Edward Dent. Its chimes were first heard on 23rd October 1858, just a few weeks before Big Ben was first heard.

Have **you** seen Big Ben?

One of Britain's finest architects of all time, Sir George Gilbert Scott, was commissioned to rebuild the Minster, which stands today as one of Doncaster's greatest attractions.

Can you spot it?

ANIMAL SPECIAL!

Yorkshire wood carver Robert Thompson is famous for carving mice in his furniture. How many can you spot inside the church?

Fact or fiction? Saint George is famous for slaying a dragon. But did this really happen? Why not look up 'Saint George' on the Internet to find out more?

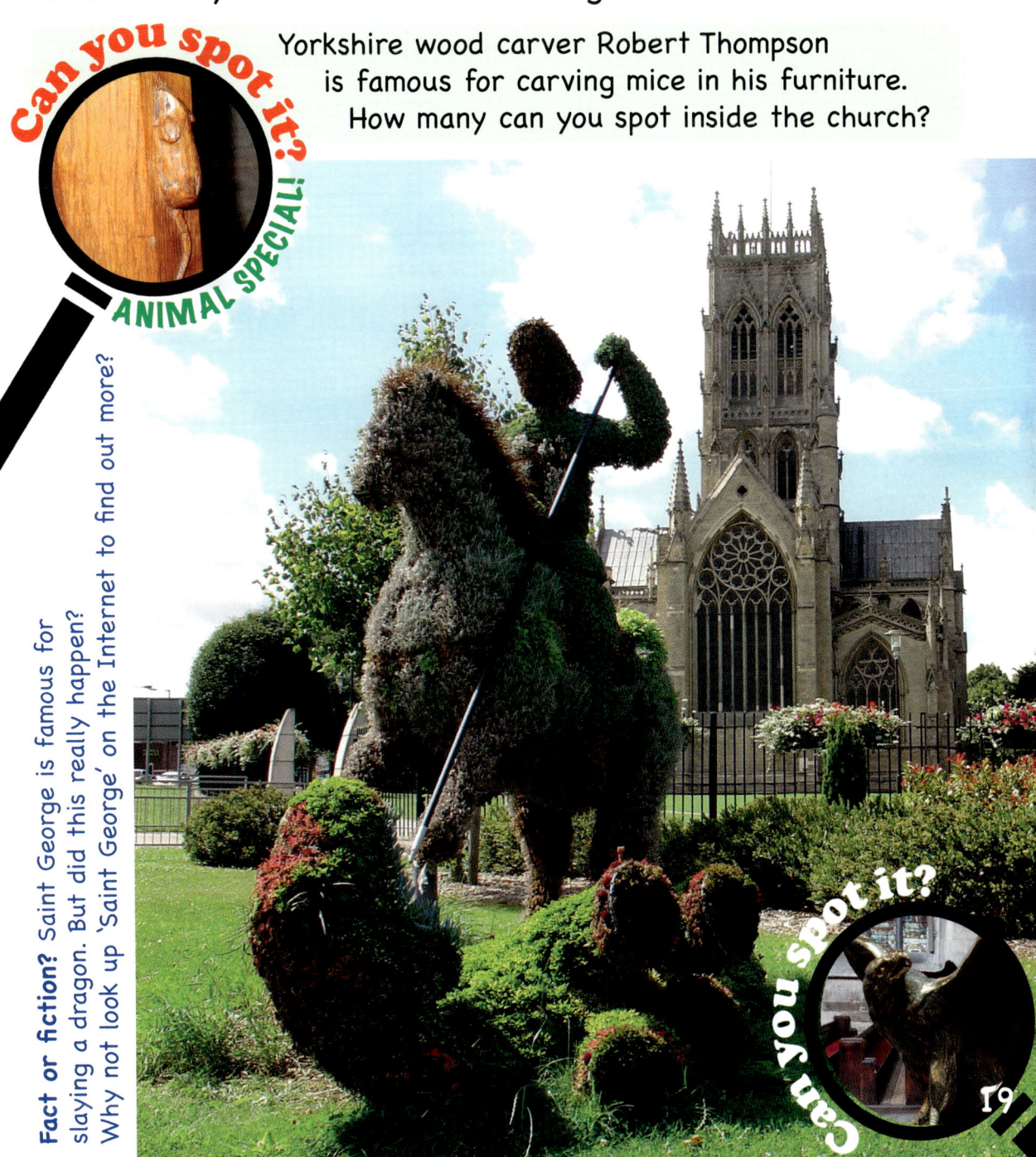

Can you spot it?

Planes, trains

Welcome to the industrial age!

Doncaster is almost exactly half-way between London and Scotland's capital, Edinburgh. It meant that our town was in the perfect position to develop transport. Some of the world's earliest planes, trains and cars were built here.

- Doncaster manufactured the Cheswold motor car, just before the first world war. You can see one today in Doncaster Museum!

- Doncaster is famous for flying! The racecourse hosted some of the world's first planes, our RAF base was home to the famous Vulcan bombers and now people can fly worldwide from Robin Hood Airport!

Can you spot it!

WELCOME TO
HEXTHORPE
HOME OF THE FLYING SCOTSMAN

The world's most famous steam trains were built in Doncaster.

Trains were built by the Great Northern Railway at the Doncaster Works, known as "The Plant" since 1853. Many of the very first steam trains were built here, including Flying Scotsman and Mallard, which reached a speed of 126 miles per hour in 1938, making it the world's fastest steam train ever!

STINKY FACT!

A stink bomb was used on Mallard's record-breaking journey. Speed was dangerous and there was a risk that the furnace might overheat. If it did, the stink bomb would crack and let the driver know to stop the train.

DISGUSTING Doncaster!

Racing Doncaster

How did Doncaster become world famous for its horse racing?

Well, remember those great roads built by the Romans? Doncaster's perfect position on the Great North Road meant that horse-drawn stage coaches stopped off on their way south at our coaching inns. With so many horses around, people naturally began to race them!

Can you spot it?

You can still see old coaching inns around Doncaster with archways like this one, inviting the horse-drawn carriages inside.

FACT! World famous cowboy Buffalo Bill rode into town with his 'Wild West' show in 1902.

The Story of the St Leger

It was 1776 at the Red Lion pub in Doncaster market-place. Anthony St Leger, an officer in the British Army, suggested a race for horses over a distance of two miles... and so the world-famous St Leger race was born, the oldest classic horserace in the world!

Today, over 60,000 people from all over the world come to Doncaster Racecourse for the St Leger. Fancy that!

Nice hat, lady!

Spot the Difference

Here are some old photographs next to pictures of the same locations in the modern day.

Can you spot how Doncaster has changed over the years? How have the buildings changed? What about the transport, the people and the clothes they wear?

High Street

Clock Corner

St George's Gate and Baxter Gate

Doncaster Railway Station

Station Road

War-time Doncaster

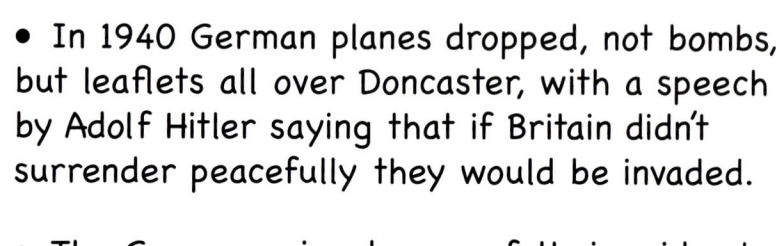

Many of Doncaster's people went to fight in the Second World War and those left behind faced hardship and **rationing**, as well as a number of air raids and bombings...

- In 1940 German planes dropped, not bombs, but leaflets all over Doncaster, with a speech by Adolf Hitler saying that if Britain didn't surrender peacefully they would be invaded.

- The Germans aimed some of their raids at the Plant works, hoping to stop us from building trains and planes to help with the war effort. Luckily, they failed.

- Doncaster's worst bombing came at midnight, 9th May 1941. Two parachute mines fell on Balby, killing 16 people and injuring 73.

Many Doncaster people were urged to 'dig for victory' and grow their own food during the war.

A young Winston Churchill visited Doncaster's Corn Exchange, telling audiences about his experiences during the Boer War.

DONCASTER STAR

Doncaster RAF pilot Sir Douglas Bader lost both his legs after a plane crash in 1931. But that didn't stop him becoming a hero! Douglas walked again using artificial legs just six months later.

When World War II was declared, Sir Douglas flew again! In his Spitfire plane, he shot down 23 enemy aircraft making him 'the fifth most deadly fighter pilot in the RAF'.

But then, disaster struck once more! Sir Douglas collided with a German fighter plane over France and was forced to bail out. He even left one of his false legs in the cockpit!

He was captured by the Germans and taken to a prisoner of war camp. There, he made friends with his captors and even persuaded them to let the British fly him over a new leg.

But cunning Sir Douglas managed to escape... quite an achievement with no real legs! Unfortunately, he was captured again and sent to Germany.

He remained as a prisoner until he was freed by American troops in 1945. Sir Douglas Bader returned to England a true hero.

FACT! During the First World War, Doncaster Racecourse was used as a base for the Royal Flying Corps fighters.

Mining

The **population** of Doncaster grew massively with the development of coal mining. Coal mines and their structures are called "collieries". Many collieries were built, along with houses for the miners and their families to live in. Of course, Doncaster's train, canal and river links helped move the coal around the country.

In the 1970s and the early 1980s, however, many of the mines were closed, leaving these people without jobs.

The town bounced back by developing its service industries, with leisure and food at Lakeside, bars in the town centre and out-of-town retail parks for shopping.

DONCASTER STAR

Arthur Wharton

Born in Ghana, Africa in 1865, Arthur Wharton moved to our area aged 19, where he became the world's first black professional football player. As goalkeeper, Wharton was a true entertainer. He would wait in a crouching position at the side of the goal before rushing out to save the ball. He called his famous move the "spider kick"

FAMOUS DONCASTER AUTHORS!

World-famous author Ted Hughes was brought up in Mexborough. Read 'The Iron Man'... it is brilliant!

Doncaster Rovers

Doncaster Rovers was formed in 1879 by Albert Jenkins, who worked at Doncaster's Great Northern Railway Works ('the Plant'). It is one of the oldest football clubs in England – older than Liverpool, Arsenal, Chelsea and many others.

Our dog is named after Donny Dog, the famous Doncaster Rovers mascot!

Doncaster Museum

Gervase Phinn is another top local author. Give his books a go... you'll love them!

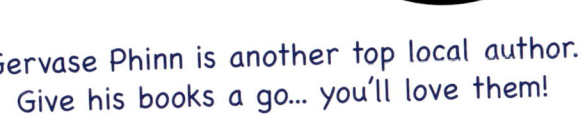

Can you spot it?

Cusworth Hall

21st Century Doncaster

We've found out that Doncaster was a very exciting place to be... and still is!

You can visit Yorkshire Wildlife Park, go shopping in the Frenchgate Centre, see a play at the Cast Theatre or have fun at The Dome.

Perhaps we'll see you there!

LEMURS ON THE LOOSE!

Oh no! Three cheeky lemurs have escaped from the Yorkshire Wildlife Park! Can you find them hiding in the pages of this book?

DONCASTER STAR

Jeremy Clarkson

Jeremy Clarkson was the presenter of 'Top Gear', the world's most watched factual TV show. He is also one of our country's best-selling writers and is known for outspoken opinions!

Glossary

Those words in **bold** explained...

AD - a short way to write "anno Domini", which is Latin for the years "after the birth of Christ".

ancestors - a person related to you from many years ago.

BC - this stands for "before Christ".

borough - a large town, divided into smaller sections

charter - a legal paper given to a town or city.

composer - someone who writes music.

continent - the world is split into seven land masses called continents.

county - a country can be divided up into various counties.

fort - a strong or fortified place occupied by soldiers and usually surrounded by walls.

habitat - the natural place for an animal to live

horse garrison - the place where troops and their horses were stationed.

industry - a business activity, usually making things to sell.

peat - a soil found in marshy or damp regions.

Pennines - a range of hills separating North West England from Yorkshire.

portcullis - a strong gate, let down to stop people entering.

rationing - a fixed allowance of food.

stocks - a device for locking a person in place as punishment.

Louis Tomlinson

DONCASTER STAR

Doncaster's Louis Tomlinson was propelled to fame when his band One Direction was formed on TV show 'The X Factor' in 2010. Louis is now famous worldwide. In 2013 he was even signed to play for Doncaster Rovers!

Index

Quiz time!

1) Is this a fiction or non-fiction book?

2) What features of the book tell you it is non-fiction?

3) Why are some words in **bold**? How does this link with the glossary?

4) See page 10: Why is Henry VIII saying "Thanks!" to the River Don?

5) See page 13: What was the keep used for at Conisborough Castle?

6) See page 15 (Horrible Doncaster): How did the Roundheads trick Colonel Rainsborough?

7) See page 17: Why do you think a block of flats was built on top of the Sandhouse tunnels? Do you think that was a good idea? Explain your answer.

8) See page 18: What has Doncaster Minster got in common with Big Ben?

9) See page 27: Why is Sir Douglas Bader's story so amazing?

10) Look through the book... which of the 'Doncaster Stars' do you most admire and why?

Discover more about the author/illustrator
and watch a video of his play 'Disgusting Doncaster' at
www.philshepp.com